The People's History

Great Lumley & Fence Houses

by Lena Cooper

Lumley Bethel Choir and some Sunday School children in 1953. The Choir
Master was Mr Tom Scott. Back row: H. Graver, A. Ramsey, R. Maddison,
J. Bellis, H. Willis, J. Hewlett, G. Graver, R. Hewitson, E. Watson, A. Graver,
R. Pimlett and H. Roughley.

Previous page: Fence Houses taxi, 1923.

Copyright © Lena Cooper 2001

First published in 2001 by

The People's History Ltd
Suite 1
Byron House
Seaham Grange Business Park
Seaham
Co. Durham
SR7 0PY

ISBN 1 902527 26 7

No part of this publication may be reproduced, stored in a mechanical retrieval
system, or transmitted, in any form or by any means, electronic, mechanical,
photocopying, recording or otherwise, without prior permission of the author.

Contents

A Fence Houses family group – the Dawson family in the early 1900s. Back row: Joseph Dawson, Mr Dawson (father) and Lance Dawson. Middle row: Jane Dawson, Robert Dawson, Mrs Dawson (mother), Ann Esther (Net) Dawson, Mary Annie Dawson and Ted Dawson. Front row: Susan Dawson, Harry Dawson and Baby Herbert Dawson (on his mother's knee).

Lena Cooper dedicates this book to the memory of Thomas Bulmer and Dorothy Bulmer with grateful thanks.

Introduction

In this book I have included a number of photographs of people whose labour, vision and enterprise helped to bring about the progress that we enjoy today. No doubt there are many more photographs of Great Lumley and Fence Houses (Little Lumley) that I have not seen but I hope that the owners of these will treasure them as a valuable asset in the history of the two villages.

Relax and enjoy the book.

Lena Cooper
Fence Houses, 2001

An aerial view of Great Lumley village taken possibly in the 1980s.

A general view of Lumley Sixth Pit.

Acknowledgements

Lena Cooper acknowledges with gratitude and sincere thanks the following people for their contribution in photographs or stories or even just encouragement, to the compilation of this book:

Mr George Atkinson, Mrs Mollie Beattie, Mr J. Burleson (Headteacher Lumley School), Miss Eleanor Carr, Mrs Irene Corner, Mrs Lilian Curry, Mrs Sheila Elliott, Mrs Jean Fenny, Mrs Eileen Fletcher (Woodlea School), Mr A.K. Garner, Mr Jimmy Gascoigne, Mr Morgan Hardy, Mr Eddie Horsely, Major James Howe MBE, LRAM, ARCM, Mr Sam Hunter, Mr Bill Ivison, Mr Tom Knox, Mrs Janet Maddison, Mr Robert Maddison, Mrs Betty Mason, Mrs Irene Naisbitt, Mrs Ella Nelson, Mr Alan Oliver, Mrs Betty Ray, Mr Tom Robson, Mr Billy Roughley, Mrs Gladys Stockdale, Mrs Nancy Sweeting, Mrs Lilian Tindale, Mrs Cath Wareham, Mrs Denise Webster, Mrs Mary Welsh, Mrs Helen Wilson and Mrs Yvonne Wilson.

Very special thanks are also due to:

Mr Andrew Clark, Mr George Nairn and Mr Geoffrey Berriman for their unfailing help and support.

Appreciation and many thanks for co-operation go to:

Beamish Archives – The North of England Open Air Museum
Northeast Press Limited, Sunderland Echo
Northern Echo
Great Lumley Community Centre

GREAT LUMLEY

General view of the rowing boat for Lumley Ferry across the River Wear at Chester-le-Street, *circa* 1904. The Ferry House is in the background.

Front Street, Great Lumley – possibly early 1920s. In the distance can be seen Christ Church spire and a herd of cattle being shepherded along the street. A bull-nose Morris car is seen on the right.

A general view of Front Street, Great Lumley 2001.

Main Street, Great Lumley – again with the photographer's car in the
background.

Main Street, Great Lumley, 2001.

The Seven Stars Public House, Great Lumley (right centre), early 1900s.

Where the Seven Stars public house used to be – Main Street, Great Lumley, 2001.

The old community centre in Lumley which closed in the early 1970s.

Council Houses, Great Lumley. 7224

A view of some Council houses at Great Lumley. Christ Church is on the right.

LAST OCCUPANT LEAVES DUCK'S HOSPITAL

Great Lumley almshouse to be demolished

Duck's Hospital, now a tumbledown building. Below: Mr. C. W. Robson (left) talking to Mr. Robert Swinney.—[N.E.]

THE last occupant of Duck's Hospital, Great Lumley, near Chester-le-Street, an almshouse founded by indenture on September 29, 1686, has just been rehoused in a council flat, and a once attractive, but now tumbledown building, an interesting relic of the old days of charitable benefaction, awaits demolition.

Duck's Hospital, as it is popularly known, derived its name from its founder, Sir John Duck, who has been called Durham's Dick Whittington.

The original foundation was "for the sustentation and relief of 12 poor, aged, and impotent people," and the first occupants of the apartment building, with its own chapel and courtyard, were one man and 11 widows. These "Brethren and Sisters of the Hospital of John Duck Esq., in the County of Durham" and their successors had, it is recorded, "a common seal with a cross graven thereon, and, in the circumference thereof, also engraven, Sigilla Hospital is John Duck Ar Apud Magna Lumley in Com. Dunelm."

Got 1s a week

The residents, "elected from the parish of Chester or the neighbourhood," each originally received 52s a year by quarterly payments. Prayers had to be said twice a day, with a sermon every Sunday in the chapel, by a minister, deacon or priest of the Church of England, who received £10 a year for "his support and maintenance."

The chapel was later made into another living apartment, but a reminder remains today in the bell on the roof of the building.

Sir John Duck retained the management of the charity and supporting estates until his death in 1691, when it passed to his wife, Dame Anne Duck, who died four ars later. In the subsequent ccession, an ancestor of Queen zabeth the Queen Mother, Lord hn Glamis, afterwards the ninth rl of Strathmore, had an interest, st of the estates were subsequently disposed of, and the arity passed to local trustees. e Earl of Durham kept the ilding in repair for a time, and o appointed the almspeople and chaplain.

85-year-old trustee

Among the final trustees is Robert Swinney, aged 85, who ll lives at Great Lumley. As he efully surveyed the dilapidated d condemned building, with its l-tiled roof and air-gun pellet les through the bottle-glass ndows, he said: "It is a link th a fine old past, but it will ve to come down I suppose. It a place of memories, and many l people have had cause to be nkful for it."

Sir John Duck founded the Almshouses popularly known as 'Duck's Hospital' at Great Lumley in 1686. Originally 'for the sustentation and relief of 12 poor, aged and impotent people', the first occupants of the apartment building, which had its own chapel and courtyard, were one man and eleven widows. This newspaper cutting from 1960 shows, after about 274 years of charitable benefaction, the dilapidated building awaits demolition, the last occupant having been rehoused in a Council flat. A reminder of the chapel, before it also was made into another dwelling area, is the bell just visible in this picture above rooftop centre.

M. Tindale's butcher shop, Lumley. Jenny Tindale (born 1912) stands outside with her mother. Jenny's father, Matthew Tindale, started the business in 1899 when he built the shop and the house next door. Matthew was called up for the First World War and the shop had to be closed. The only boy in the family, Jenny's brother Jack, was too young to serve in the shop. The business reopened after the war and later made soup for the villagers during the 1926 Strike.

A modern view of Great Lumley Post Office, 2001. This was originally M. Tindale's butcher shop.

The local doctor's surgery, Front Street, Great Lumley, 2001.

The Warriors Arms public house, Great Lumley, 2001.

Lumley Bethel Chapel, *circa* 1980.

The foundation for the new Methodist Church with the old Bethel Chapel in the background on the right, *circa* 1988.

Lumley Methodist Chapel. The old chapel dates from 1786. In 1821 the addition of a gallery along with other improvements was made, thus enlarging the chapel which was originally a typical early Methodist meeting house built more for its usefulness than for its beauty. However, it was pulled down and replaced by a more modern building which was opened for public worship in 1906. The building is now, in 2001, no longer a chapel, having been purchased privately for other purposes.

The New Lumley Methodist Church, Front Street, Great Lumley, 2001. The main section of the church was opened on 16th July 1988 by Mr Paul G. Bartlett Lang who represented the Joseph Rank Benevolent Trust. Mr David Myles was the architect. The local minister was Rev John L.H. Allison, who received the key on behalf of the local church. The second section of the church was opened on 9th January 1999.

Christ Church, Great Lumley as viewed from the Front Street, Lumley.

Another view of Front Street, Great Lumley, 2001. The Dog and Gun public house is centre left and the spire of Christ Church, Great Lumley can be seen centre right.

A view of Christ Church, Lumley, showing the Lych Gate entrance from the main road, *circa* 1990.

Side view of Christ Church, Lumley, showing some of the old headstones, *circa* 1990.

Notice Board at Christ Church, Lumley, *circa* 1990.

This 'Oliver' headstone in Christ Church burial ground reads as follows:

'In memory of the beloved son and daughter of Henry and Margaret Oliver. Ann Oliver died at 6 Pit Sept 16th 1870 aged 2 years and 10 months. Joseph Oliver died at 6 Pit Dec 21st 1872 aged 7 years. And the parents gave in tears and pain The flowers they most did love They know they should find them all again In the fields of light above. Also of Joseph Smith Oliver, son of the above who died at 6th Pit 2nd Feb 1880 aged 6 years. The above Henry Oliver, husband of Margaret Oliver, born Sept 10th 1842 died Feb 15th 1919. Also the above Margaret Oliver who died June 27th 1938 aged 91 years. Also son of the above, Henry Oliver who died 11th Dec 1946 aged 64 years.

(The Monumental Stonemason was J. Kell.)

Roll of Honour for the First World War (1914 to 1918) at the Lych Gate, Christ Church, Lumley.

Roll of Honour for the Second World War (1939 to 1945) at the Lych Gate, Christ Church, Lumley.

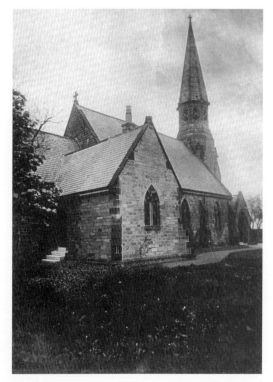

A view of Christ Church, Great Lumley. A postcard sent in 1908.

FENCE HOUSES

Mr George Carr of Co-operative Terrace, Fence Houses with Mr Thomas (Tommy) Anderson of Morton Crescent pose together, both having reached the age of 50. Tommy used to deliver 'Yeast' to the residents of Fence Houses.

Emma Charlton gets some fresh air at the open doorway of her house at Wood Row, Woodstone Village, Fence Houses. The houses in Wood Row have long since been demolished.

Dorothy Bulmer with four of her grandchildren in the backyard of 18 Briarwood Street, Fence Houses, *circa* 1927. Left to right: Billy Dawson, Lena Dawson, Elsie Dawson, Dorothy and Ronnie Maddison (cousin).

Mr and Mrs John Stark with their children Denis and Doris take a break from their walk up Morton Drive, Fence Houses, in the 1940s. Many years later Denis owned the DIY business at Shiney Row.

Young cousins Doris Stark (standing) and Edna Stark (seated) in the front garden of 18 Briarwood Street, Fence Houses, *circa* 1936.

Sisters Lisa and Melissa Dawson have some snowballing fun up Morton Drive, Fence Houses, in 1984.

The slope of Morton Drive – perfect for sledging – 1984.

The beauty of Nature – Wintry scene near the entrance to Morton Drive in 1984.

Even Grandad's at it! Winter snow in 1984.

The Dun Cow Inn, Fence Houses, March 1980.

Cedarwood Estate, Fence Houses, was built to house Senior Citizens of the village. The houses are on one level and built in blocks of four. The total number of houses is 17 (including the house adjoining Cedarwood Communal Hall).

Another view showing the Cedarwood Communal Hall (front right), the top end of Finchale Terrace (right background) and (centre background) part of High Row in 1997.

A view of Morton Wood (background) taken from Cedarwood in 1997. Just left of centre can be seen Morton Cottage.

From Cedarwood another view of the fields showing Morton Grange Farm in the background, right of centre.

The front of Sydney Street, Fence Houses facing across the 'Sports Day' playing field of Lambton School's.

SCHOOLDAYS

Lollipop Man, Mr George Lodge, escorts Lumley Schoolchildren safely across busy roads in October 1967.

A pre-11-plus girls class at Fence Houses Junior School celebrating 'British Empire Day' (24th May) in the schoolyard, *circa* 1930.

Doreen Yellowley in 1939. Fence Houses Senior and Junior School.

Fence Houses schoolgirls, Standard 4/5 on a trip to Seaton Carew, 1932. In the centre is their teacher, Miss Minnie Bolton.

Fence Houses Junior Mixed School, Class 2, 1949, with Mr Kirkbride (Headmaster) on the right (seated) and Mr Gascoigne (Teacher) on the left.

Fence Houses Junior Mixed School, Class 4, 1949. Mr Kirkbride (Headmaster) is seated on the right.

School gymnasts at Fence Houses Secondary Modern School, April 1949.

Fence Houses School swimmers with Mr D. Bland, August 1949.

Fence Houses Secondary Modern School Prize Winners, November 1952.

A presentation of a clock to Mr Gleadhill, Headmaster of Fence Houses Modern School, on his retirement, October 1950.

Children from Fence Houses Senior and Junior Mixed School on a school trip in 1958. Photograph shows Miss Mason, Beryl Mills, Christine Crawley, Yvonne Charlton and Veronica Garden.

Fence Houses Junior Mixed School in the early 1960s. A lot of recognisable faces on this one.

A class of girls at Lumley School with their teacher, possibly early 1900s.

Lumley Council School, Boys Department in 1922. In first row standing are Wilf Fenny, first left and Bobby Moody, second left.

Wilfred Fenny with his wife Doris and son Alan, *circa* 1940. Wilfred was caretaker at Lumley Junior school for many years as was his father (Herbert Fenny) before him. Doris also served the school as a dinner lady. Alan grew up to be of invaluable help in the running of Lumley Juniors football team for many years.

Boys aged between 5 and 6 years of age at Lumley Boys School, 1927. Included in the photograph are: Tommy Thompson, Alf Stockdale (next to teacher in second row), Maurice Pile and George Coulter.

Lumley Schools Boys Football Team, 1965-66. They were C.B. Watson Cup-Winners and League Runners-up. Back left is Mr Garner (Headteacher), back right is Mr (Ollie) Willis, front left is not known and front right is Mr Colin Frederickson.

Lumley Junior Mixed School Boys Football Team, 1978-79.

Lumley School Girls Netball Team, 1971-72.

Lumley School dinner ladies and nannies with Mr George Lodge (Lollipop Man) and Mr A.K. Garner (Headmaster) in the 1970s. Standing: Mr Lodge, Audrey Grey, Ella Smith and Mr A.K. Garner. Seated: Edith Hulme, Nancy Allon, Doris Fenny, Lizzie Hall and Jean Fenny.

It is worth mentioning here that Mr A.K. Garner was headmaster at Lumley School for 19 years from 1965 – 1984 and achieved much for the school. The villagers hold him in high regard. Well done sir.

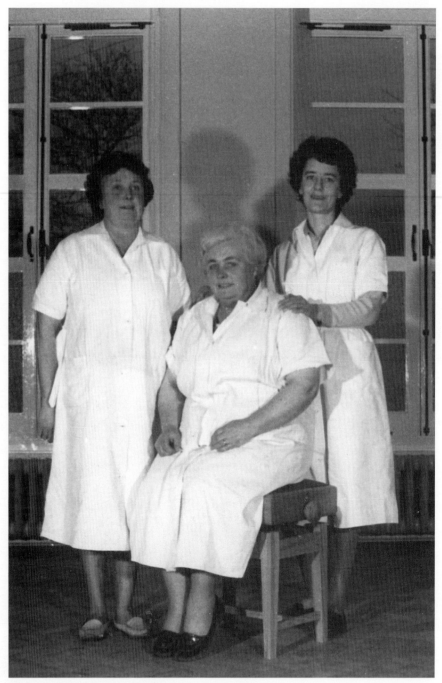

Three of the dinner ladies at Lumley School. Left to right: Lizzie Hall, Doris Fenny and Gwennie Ramshaw.

Lumley Junior School Staff,
1987. Back row: J. Chapman
(Secretary), C. Wareham,
J. Taylor, E, Gilderoy. Front row:
J. Phetonby, M. Smith (Deputy
Head), S. Proctor (Head) and
R. Knight.

After 32 years as school
caretaker at Lumley Cocken
Lane Junior School, Wilfred
Fenny hands over his sweeping
brush in 1978 to (from front):
Clair Wilson, Geoffrey
Robinson, Christopher Hunter,
Julie Thompson, Gillian
Milburn and John Huntley.
Wilfred succeeded his father
Herbert Fenny who was
caretaker when the school
opened in 1931 until 1946.

Lumley Bethel Sunday Schoolchildren. The teachers were: Mrs J. Bell and Mrs
C. Taite. Yvonne Richardson, Dorothy Brown and George Roughley are at the
front of the group.

Lumley Bethel Sunday School Anniversary, *circa* 1948. Back row: Mary Curry,
Enid Roughley, Jean Bell, Hazel Thompson, Mary Maddison and Phyllis Hewit.
Also included are: Margaret Scott, Joyce Roughley, Brenda Pimlett and Marian
Bell.

Children of Woodlea Primary Nursery School, 1989. The group includes: Mrs Falcus, Mrs Coulthard, Miss Wilson, Gary Sulkiviez, Nathan Orrell, Gary Turnbull, Adrian Mitchell, Brian Ridley, Simon Proud, Emma Lowden, Clare Boster, Lucy Ray, Gemma Henderson, Fiona Johnson, Kay Wilson, Lisa Maddison, Clare Griffin and Clare Bell.

Woodlea School Nursery Class – 2000. Back row: Miss Claire Beedham, Rebecca Coates, David Armstrong, Stephanie Todd, Abby Donkin, Michael Williamson, Jack Asbery and Mrs Val Mudd. Middle row: Connor Robson, Beth Maddison, Jordan Sutherland, Charlotte Pilsworth, Caitlin Kyle, Arron Dickinson, Joseph Telford and Elliott Pearson. Front row: Jed Stoker, Laura Passmoor, Lee Pearson, Andrew Hern, Kieron Brown, Sean Tindale, Bethany Foster, Stephanie Passmoor and Peter Hayes.

Woodlea School Girls Netball Team in the 1970s. Back Row: Elaine Banks (Teacher), Lyndsey Davison, Sharon Smith, Deborah Taylor and Lisa Douglas. Front row: Moira Blackbird, Tracey Naisbitt, Sharon Fisher, Amanda Woodhead and Cheryl Smith.

It's party time! Woodlea schoolchildren celebrate the Silver Jubilee of Her Majesty Queen Elizabeth II's Accession to the Throne in 1977.

An 'Indian Pageant' performed by Woodlea schoolchildren in 1977.

Woodlea Primary School Prize Day, *circa* 1979. Includes: Mark Smith, Adam Wilson, Graham Walton, David Bell, Alan Wise, Andrew Dickinson, Craig Cumpson, Deborah Taylor, Judith Chater, Samantha and Alison Jones, Tara Patterson, Lynn Hood, Deborah Walker, Sharon Neesam, Mr Jack Davison (Headteacher), Lindsay Davison, Sharon Smith, Alex Boyle, David Robson and Malcolm Passmoor.

Proudly displaying their Cups and Medals, Woodlea School Boys Football Team, 1980-81. Team: Darren Todd, Billy Earlie, Glen White, Steven Ranson, Adrian Fletcher, Mark Smith, Robert Chapplow, Elliott Patterson, Paul Conn, Graham Walton, Joseph Highley, Craig Cumpson, Scott Starke, Simon Cossar and Peter Birtwisle (Teacher and Coach).

Woodlea Primary School Boys Football Team, 1982-83. Included in the group are: Gary Cumpson, Andrew Slack, Craig Fisher, Stephen Lovick, Paul Conn, James Robson, Darren Arthur, Ian Hall, Simon Cossor, Paul Fletcher, Ian Robson, Ian Storey and Craig Patterson.

Children of Woodlea Junior School in the playground, July 1989. Briarwood Street (background right) and (top left) part of the temporary building which replaced the brick building previously built there for the Juniors.

Woodlea Juniors enjoy their game while sports teacher looks on in 1989. Far background is Gill Crescent South and in the front of that street is School Terrace.

A Woodlea Primary School Class, 1990. Includes: Sam Hinton, Dean Cockburn, James Henderson, Shaun Brown, Alan Conn, Nigel Bailey, Christopher Beattie, Martin Lewins, Andrew Brumby, Emma Gatt, Joanne Mansfield, Stephen Round, David Sayers, Christopher Hall, Victoria Falcus, Shane Cummings, Adam Daines, Simon Proud, Faye Kennedy and Mr Watson (Teacher).

AT WORK

A group of miners with friends and families in front of the Lumley 6th Pit Colliery, proudly holding their Lodge Banner in the late 1950s.

A very rare photograph of Lumley Colliery (not to be confused with Lumley Sixth Pit Colliery) which was situated some distance behind Christ Church, Great Lumley. It is thought to have closed in the mid 1800s.

General view of colliery yard and railway sidings at Lumley Sixth Pit, Fence Houses in the 1950s.

Lumley Sixth Pit Colliery – a view from the main road, Fence Houses in the early 1960s.

Mr Arthur McKitten with a Colliery Horse (Blackie) at Lumley Sixth Pit.

Lumley Sixth Pit Colliery Baths were opened by Mr Austin Kirkup in February 1939.

A group of Fence Houses people at the opening of Sixth Pit Colliery Baths.

With a record of 58 years service at Lumley Sixth Pit Mr Charles Carr of Lumley Thicks is presented with a Pit Lamp as the oldest ex-miner along with the youngest miner who also received a lamp. In the background the Colliery Manager, Mr Stan Stokoe, looks on in this late 1940s photograph.

Mr Sam Watson of the National Union of Mineworkers presenting Mrs Margaret Middlemass with a medallion in recognition of services rendered to the NUM by her late husband Mr Edward (Ned) Thomas Middlemass in the 1960s. The photograph was taken at Sixth Pit Welfare Hall.

Tubs at the 'P' Drift, Lumley Sixth Pit.

Two miners leaving the 'P' Drift.

The front and back of NUM Lumley Sixth Pit Lodge Banner, 1961. The Banner was new in 1960. The illustration is entitled: 'Time shall come when war shall cease, when swords shall be beaten into ploughshares and spears into pruning hooks – then Union shall prevail.' The Colliery closed in 1966. This banner was acquired by Morrison Busty Lodge.

DMA Lumley Lodge Banner at the 70th Durham Miners' Gala, 18th July 1953. The illustration, depicting the Lion and Lamb lying down together, is entitled: 'The Reign of Peace.'

The Lodge Banner being carried by miners of the Lumley Sixth Pit through the main street of Fence Houses in the late 1950s.

Fence Houses veteran miners receive diplomas from Sam Watson, of the NUM (Durham), in October 1953.

Lambton Miners and supporters grouped around the Lambton Lodge Banner, 22nd July 1950. Lambton D Colliery closed in 1965.

Wooden waggonway track excavated at the site of Lambton D Pit in 1996.

Ford Cottage – The manager of Lumley Brickworks paid a peppercorn rent to live here.

Employees of Lumley Brickworks are guests of Lady Serena Lambton at her home in Scarborough in 1978. Included are: Jenny Porter, Alan Beattie, Cilla Blackburn, Mr Coggins (Managing Director), Gordon Walker, Bert Elliott, Stella Blackburn, Colin Sanderson, George Little, James Garside, George McCormack, Audrey McCormack and Jack Maguire. Lady Serena is on the second step.

A view of Lumley Brickworks. In the background can just be seen the roofs of High Row and behind them the chimney pots of Finchale Terrace. To the left and just visible is the Miners' Institute and Welfare Hall at Sixth Pit – later known as Woodstone Village, Fence Houses. The site of the Brickworks has since been developed into an estate of private dwelling houses in the late 1990s.

A Huwood Conveyor feeding seggar to the Pug Mill at Lumley Brickworks, Fence Houses.

Employees of Isaac Berriman, Builder, Fence Houses.

The only garage workshop in Fence Houses, July 1950. From left to right: Lambton Storey, Bill Curry, Tom Curry (garage owner) Fred Colwill and David Pringle.

Hunter's bus ran from Lumley to Rainton and Chester-le-Street. Driver Alfie Cowan is on the left and conductor Johnny Hunter on the right in 1938.

Northern Bus Company fitters, *circa* 1945. In the back row is Tommy Robson who trained as a mechanic at the Northern Garage and went on to open his own garage at Great Lumley.

Presentation of a clock being made by Mr R.E. Purvis, *circa* 1900. Mr Purvis was the first secretary and treasurer of the Lumley, Burnmoor and Fence Houses Nursing Association, 1898-1910.

Nurse DAVISON, 1901-1905

Queen's Nurse FARQUHARSON, 1910-1922

Nurse HAY, 1922-1924

Nurse BINKS, 1924-1929

Past nurses of the Nursing Association who worked in Great Lumley from 1901 to 1948: Nurse Davison, 1901-05; Queen' Nurse Farquharson, 1910-22; Nurse Hay, 1922-24; Nurse Binks, 1924-29, Queen's Nurse Jones, 1928-48.

A corner of the modernised Grocery Department of Fence Houses branch of the Chester-le-Street Co-operative Society Ltd, *circa* 1937. Showing to the right - Mr George Carr (in charge) and to the left Mr John (Jack) Pratt who usually served on the bacon section.

A photo taken in the back yard of the Fence Houses branch of the Co-op, showing Mr J. Hutchinson, driver of the delivery wagon, with on his knee Lena Dawson, young drapery assistant. To the right (standing) is Mr George Carr, centre is Mr Harry Hamilton (grocery section) and left is Mr Jimmy Green, head of the butchery section, *circa* 1937.

Jack Pratt in his special place behind the bacon counter of the Fence Houses branch of the Chester-le-Street Co-operative Society Ltd, *circa* 1937.

Young men of Great Lumley. From left to right: W. Swinney (haulage), J.W. Tindale (butcher), Adam Elliott (farmer) and W. Curry (butcher).

Robert Wilson (Senior) and Robert Wilson (Junior) by their butchers cart at Fence Houses in 1930s.

J.C. Wilkinson worked in this butcher's shop at Fence Houses from 1929 until 1973 – 44 years, almost a lifetime – then he retired and Robert Twinn took over. It was always a pleasure to shop there (the name above the shop was never changed) but everything comes to an end and in 1999 the decision was made to close the shop. It was retirement time for Robert (Bobby) Twinn and his colleague Fred Bray. Together they served Fence Houses people (and others) for a total of 26 years. Well done to all of you who worked and served in this sadly missed establishment.

Robert Twinn and Fred Bray behind the counter of the butchers shop on its last day of business in 1999.

Robert Twinn, his sister Sheila Elliott and Fred Bray stand outside of the butchers shop on the last day of business.

Charles Clarkson Curry (1887-1914), a Lumley butcher, standing outside of his shop, *circa* 1913. Beside the horse is his brother, John Grant Curry (1895-1956) and on the seat of the cart is Charles' son, John Clarkson Curry (1909-1959).

Michael McKitten who helped out at Tindale's butcher shop at Lumley, standing beside the horse and butchers cart, *circa* 1927.

Matthew Tindale and beast behind Tindale's butchers shop.

A. Elliott and sons of Middle
Farm, Lumley with horse and
rolley at a show – probably in
the Lumley area.

Members of the Elliott family
who farmed at Lumley.

Adam Elliott harrowing at Lumley Farm.

Billy Robinson ploughing near Lumley, with Jack Elliott (the farmer) looking on.

Morton Acre Farm, Fence Houses, with Steam Sentinel Car of the LNER on the Leamside to Fence Houses line.

A cart from McLaren's farm, near Lumley Thicks.

Edward Charlton gives a cheerful smile while lending a hand at Floaters Mill Farm, Fence Houses in 1940.

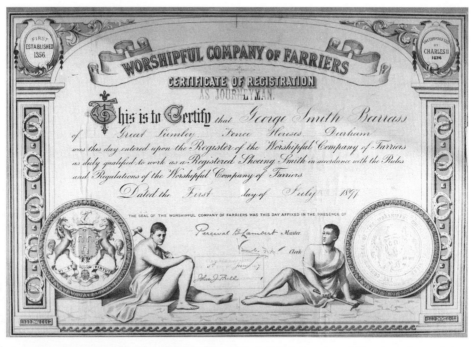

A registration Certificate for the Worshipful Company of Farriers issued to George Smith Barrass of Great Lumley, July 1897.

AT PLAY

Little Lumley Carnival outside of the Station Hotel, September 1951.

Lumley Bethel Band, *circa* 1970. The band members included: C. Maddison, D. Maddison Jnr, D. McKelwaith, A. Ramsey Jnr, A. Graver, G. Graver, A. Brown, J, Howlet, E. Roughley, R. Maddison, T. Sterling, D. Maddison, L. Maddison, L. Maddison Jnr, T. Scott, D. Roughley, R. Harrison, G. Brown, W. Roughley, D. Harrison, R. Hewitson, H. Dixon. Centre front: A. Ramsey (Bandmaster) and H. Roughley.

Lumley Colliery and Township Silver Band at the Miners' Strike Sports, Lambton, 23rd March 1912.

Lumley Colliery Silver Prize Band with the 'Cassell's Shield' at Crystal Palace 29th September 1928.

Lumley Colliery Band taken at Durham 'Big Meeting', *circa* 1930. The young lad behind the drum is Jimmy Howe who went on to become Major James Howe, MBE, LRAM, ARCM, Senior Director of Music of the Brigade of Guards (Household Division). Jimmy was born at Penshaw.

Lumley Sixth Pit Colliery Welfare Football Club in the mid 1930s. Members of the Houghton and District League since 1929 and Runners-up three times. They joined the Wearside League in the Season 1934-35 and won the Championship in 1935-36. Back row:

G. Brown (Trainer), J. Lynne (Treasurer), J. Lamb, J. Fletcher (Captain), L. Ray, C. Stoddart, J. Ramshaw, H. Brown, G. Lawson, J. Meek (Secretary) and G. Lowary. Front row: R. Tait, W. Wilkes, T. Timm, P. Fennick, E. Shaw, M. Burnham, H. Widdrington and J. Bridges (Linesman).

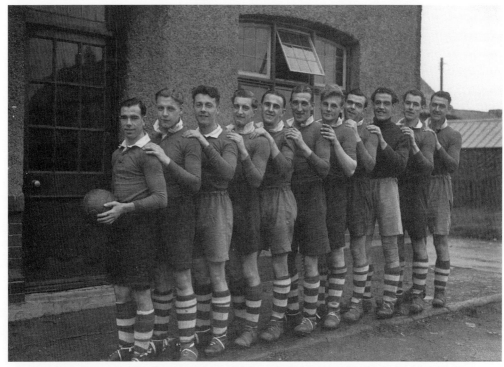

Lumley Rovers outside the Warriors Arms, Lumley, in the late 1940s. From front to back: Eddie Nicholson, Ronnie Edwards, George Peart, Leslie Sanderson, Raymond Brown, Dickie Harrison, Maurice Pyle, Eddie Horsley, Ronnie Calvert, Joe Kay and Billy Stobbs.

Married men from the Burnside Workingmen's Club, Fence Houses, take to the Burnside playing field for a game of football on Easter Monday, 1950.

Lumley Juniors AFC, 1958-59.

Well supported – Lumley AFC with the Chester-le-Street AM Cup in the 1950s.

Lumley Rovers – winners of the Birtley LCC and Chester-le-Street Aged Miners' Cups and runners-up of the Birtley Aged Miners' Cup, 1950-51.

Three Lumley footballers. Left to right: Eddie Wilson, Herbert Willis and Charlie Walt.

Cup winners outside of the Warriors Arms, Great Lumley. In the group are: R. Pyle, Mick Horsley, R. Hughes, J. Horsley, T. Green, J. Cornell and W. Edwards. Was this a bowls team?

DAYS TO REMEMBER

Golden Wedding group of James and Jane Ivison and family, *circa* 1953. Back row: Eileen Moore, Jenny Cooper, Lily Cooper, Norma Ivison, George Ivison Jnr, Joyce Ivison, Bill Ivison and Marion Ivison. Middle row: Jack Moore, Fred Cooper, Eddie Cooper, Enid Ivison, Doris Ivison, Emily Ivison and John Ivison. Front row: Nancy Ivison, Belle Moore, Sarah Cooper, James Ivison, Jane Ivison, George Ivison, James Ivison Jnr and Harry Ivison.

Great Lumley
District and Parish Council
ELECTION.

There's BOBBY with his papers,
    And PURVES with his pen;
    RENWICK for the Owners,
    And Others for the men.

Be careful what you do men,
    But do the thing that's right;
There's RENWICK, LEE, and BOBBY BURNS,
    Vote for them outright.

At RENWICK, BURNS, and LEE,
    Some will surely scoff;
Vote for them and you will see
    The Smile that wont come off.

Who was it got the Telephone?
    Why BOBBY the Paper man
And if you want the Tramways,
    He'll do the best he can.

When coming home from Chester,
    Whether sober, or you're tight;
You'll find the Bridge is closed to you
    At half-past ten at night.

And this you should not tolerate;
    The Bridge, it should be free;
To do this trick, to Poll go quick,
Vote for RENWICK, BURNS, and LEE.

And when the Summer's ended,
    And it is dark at night;
These Candidates I mention
    May get Electric Light.

Now, go to the Poll on Monday,
    With these Three on your mind;
Place a   X   beside their names,
    And they'll get in you'll find.

And when they are in, they'll work you see,
    To benefit each man;
They'll mend your roads, reduce your tolls,
    If possibly they can.

                LUMLEY ELECTOR.

S. Sedge, PRINTER, NEW LAMBTON.

A poem composed by a Lumley elector for the Great Lumley District and Parish Council Election in the early 1900s.

First World War Victory bonfire at Lumley in 1919.

Lumley folk carrying 'dolls' to help collect money for the miners – believed to be in the 1920s.

St John Ambulance Brigade (Men's Section) parade at Lumley Castle.

St John Ambulance Brigade (Women's Section) also at Lumley Castle.

A group of Salvation Army ladies at a Garden Party held at the Castle in 1931.

Hard-working Salvation Army ladies dispensing tea from urns at a Garden Party in Lumley Castle grounds in 1931.

The Duke and Duchess of York (the future King and Queen Mother) and other guests who stayed with Mr & Mrs Roger Lumley at Lumley Castle in the mid 1930s. Standing: Lord Brabourne, the Hon Thomas Coke (Equerry to the Duke), Lord Glamis, the Duke of York, Mr Roger Lumley, the Hon Robert James and Lord Barnard. Seated: Lady Brabourne, Lady Barnard, Mrs Lumley, the Duchess of York, Lady Serena James, Lady Helen Graham (Lady-in-Waiting to the Duchess).

LAUNCH OF H.M.S. "YORK"
AT JARROW.
17th JULY, 1928.

T.R.H. The Duke & Duchess of York

LEAVE LUMLEY CASTLE	2·15 p.m.
ARRIVE END OF NEW ROAD, MONKTON ...	2·37 p.m.
Alight and cut ribbon declaring road open under the name of "York Avenue." (No address or introductions or inspection of Territorials). The Jarrow Corporation Party will enter Cars and follow the Duke of York's Car to the Works.	
LEAVE FOR PALMERS WORKS, JARROW ...	2·40 p.m.
ARRIVE AT PALMERS WORKS RECEPTION ROOM	2·45 p.m.
Reception by the Directors of Palmers and their wives and Principal Admiralty Officials.	
LEAVE RECEPTION ROOM FOR WORKS ...	3·0 p.m.
The Royal Naval Volunteers will be drawn up on one side of the entrance to the Yard, and the Royal Engineers Territorial Company will be drawn up on the other side of the road at the Yard Entrance. No inspection necessary. Inspect Engines of H.M.S. "York" and proceed to Launching Platform.	
RECEIVE AN ADDRESS FROM THE MAYOR AND CORPORATION OF JARROW ...	3·15 p.m.
ARRIVE AT LAUNCHING PLATFORM	3·20 p.m.
PHOTOGRAPHING LAUNCH GROUP	3·25 p.m.
COMMENCE RELIGIOUS CEREMONY	3·30 p.m.
FINISH RELIGIOUS CEREMONY	3·40 p.m.
NAMING CEREMONY	3·43 p.m.
LAUNCH OF VESSEL	3·45 p.m.
PROCEED TO MOULD LOFT FOR REFRESHMENTS	3·50 p.m.
COMMENCEMENT WITH TOAST LIST	4·15 p.m.
(The Toast List will be cut down to occupy 30 minutes).	
FINISH TOAST LIST	4·45 p.m.
LEAVE MOULD LOFT FOR CAR	4·50 p.m.
CAR TO LEAVE WORKS	5·0 p.m.
CAR TO REACH LUMLEY CASTLE	5·30 p.m.

The Duke and Duchess of York often stayed at Lumley on their visits to the North East. Here is their itinerary for their visit in 1928 when they launched the ship, HMS *York*, at Palmer's Shipyard in Jarrow.

A Lumley party for evacuees, January 1941.

A party for Fence Houses Home Guards, January 1942.

Little Lumley pensioners enjoying their annual treat in Lumley Sixth Pit Colliery Welfare Hall. Possibly this was Christmastime 1949/50.

Great Lumley Women's Institute Concert Party in the 1950s. Back row: Maisie Tones, Betty Fenny, Winnie Moorhead, Edith Curry, Celia Patterson and Thelma Ryans. Front row: Bessie Henderson, Florrie Fenwick, Renee Green, Jennie Milford and Ena Doxford.

A visit of HRH The Princess Royal to Fence Houses YMCA, November 1954.

HRH The Princess Royal looks at the plan for the new YMCA building at Fence Houses during her visit in November 1954.

A St John Ambulance competition held at Lumley, December 1955.

Great Lumley WI Concert Party in the 1950s. Left to right: Thelma Ryans, Florrie Fenwick, Maisie Tones, Milly Pricket, Eva Brown and Bessie Henderson.

Fence Houses schoolchildren return from London in June 1949.

Fence Houses schoolchildren off to Switzerland in 1951.

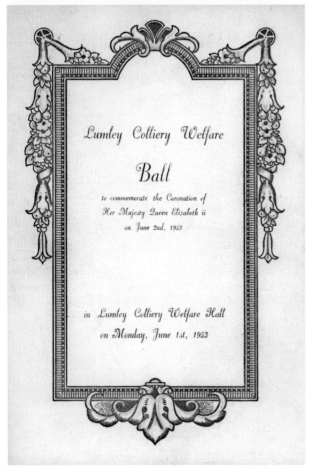

Lumley Colliery Welfare

Ball

to commemorate the Coronation of
Her Majesty Queen Elizabeth ii
on June 2nd, 1953

in Lumley Colliery Welfare Hall
on Monday, June 1st, 1953

Lumley Terrace street party to celebrate the Coronation of Queen Elizabeth II on 2nd June 1953. On the left side of the photograph are: Madge Bellis, Betty Watson, Mrs Graver, Mrs Maddison, Mrs Roughley, Raymond and Ann Johnson and Freda Graver. On the right side are: Iris Fisher, Audrey Johnson, Amelia Brown, Alice Bellis, Mr A. Graver, Joyce Graver, Thomas Fisher and Derek Graver.

A copy of an invitation to Lumley Colliery Welfare Ball to commemorate the Coronation of Her Majesty Queen Elizabeth II on 2nd June 1953 in Lumley Colliery Welfare Hall on Monday, 1st June 1953.

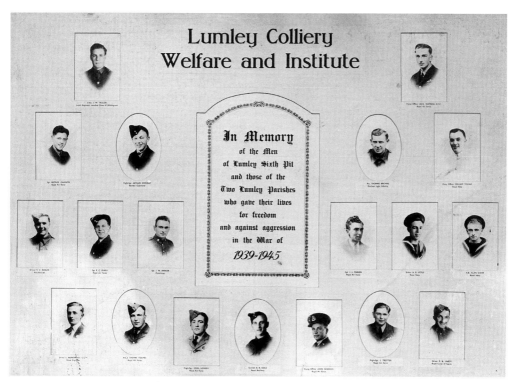

Lumley Colliery Welfare and Institute. In memory of the men of Lumley Sixth Pit and those of the two Lumley Parishes who gave their lives for freedom and against aggression in the Second World War. Top row: Lieut J.W. Taylor, Loyal Regiment, attached Duke of Wellington; Flying Officer Jack Watson DFC, Royal Air Force. Second row from top: Sgt George Johnson, Royal Air Force; Flight Sgt Arthur Swinney, Bomber Command; Pte Thomas Brown, Durham Light Infantry; Petty Officer William Young, Royal Navy. Third row from top: Driver T.V. Pascoe, Anti-Aircraft; Sgt E.C. Duffy, Royal Air Force; Sgt J.W. Parker, Paratroops; Cpl J.L. Parker, Royal Air Force; Stoker A.B. Little, Royal Navy; A.B. Alan Conn, Royal Navy. Bottom row: Driver S. Armstrong GCM, Royal Engineers; Aircraftsman Second Class Thomas Holmes, Royal Air Force; Flight Sgt John Lowery, Royal Air Force; Gunner R.B. Cole, Royal Artillery; Flying Officer John Renwick, Royal Air Force; Flight Sgt J. Trotter, Royal Air Force; Driver E.B. Vardy, Royal Corps of Signals.

Opposite page:

Lumley Sixth Pit Colliery Institute. To the Memory of our Comrades who made the supreme sacrifice in the First World War.

Lest we forget.
That Right will always conquer Might,
That Freedom might Flourish on the Earth,
That Peace and Goodwill shall prevail amongst all people,
That Military Despotism and Tyranny shall perish,
For these things in the glory and joy of young manhood,
These Comrades of ours Died.

Top line:
Gr. D. Lawson, RFA – killed October 31st 1918, France.
Pte Jos Hutchinson, NF – died of wounds November 2nd 1916, Salonica.
2nd Lieut Hugh Carr, 172nd Comp RE – died of wounds January 23rd 1916, St Eldi.
Lieut George Ernest Harker, RFA – killed in action May 19th 1917 – Arras. He served $2^1/_2$ years in France.
Pte Ed Pimlett, DLI – killed in action June 4th 1916, Somme.
Pte Thomas Hutchinson, Royal Insk D Guards – killed in action May 20th 1917, Cambria.

Second line:
Pte George L. Nelson, RFA – killed in action September 29th 1918, Burloun Forrest, France.
Pte Ralph Minto, Scottish Borders – died of wounds January 1st 1916, Salonica.
Pte Jos Pimlett, RFA – killed in action May 3rd 1917, Arras France.
Pte William Lowerson, DLI – killed in action September 22nd 1917, France.
Bandsman Thomas Tulip, DLI – killed July 19th 1916, Morlan Court, Somme.
Pte Edward Welsh, EY – killed July 8th 1916 – Trones Wood, Somme.

Third line:
Pte J.T. Appleby, DLI – died November 4th 1918, Staples, France.
L/Cpl John Trotter, DLI – killed September 20th 1916 – High Wood, Somme.
Pte Newrick Curry, DLI – killed March 3rd 1917, Heburterne Trench, France.
Dr Mark Lowerson, RFA – died December 16th 1918, Salonica.
Sergt William Meek Willis, DLI – died of wounds September 5th 1918, Messines, France.
Pte Thomas Hall, DLI – died of wounds November 16th 1916 – No 10 CCS, France.

Bottom line
Pte Jos Blenkiron, DLI – killed November 4th 1916 – France.
Corp Thomas Oliver, DLI – killed in action April 25th 1915, France.
Pte Henry Lowerson, RE – killed October 17th 1917 – Ypres Road, France.
Pte John Lowerson, DLI – killed March 24th 1918 – Mezieries.
Gr John Carr, RFA – died October 13th 1916 – Salonica.
Pte Robin Blenkiron, DLI – killed April 25th 1915 – France.
Pte Fred Stevenson, DLI – killed in action October 1st 1916 – Somme.

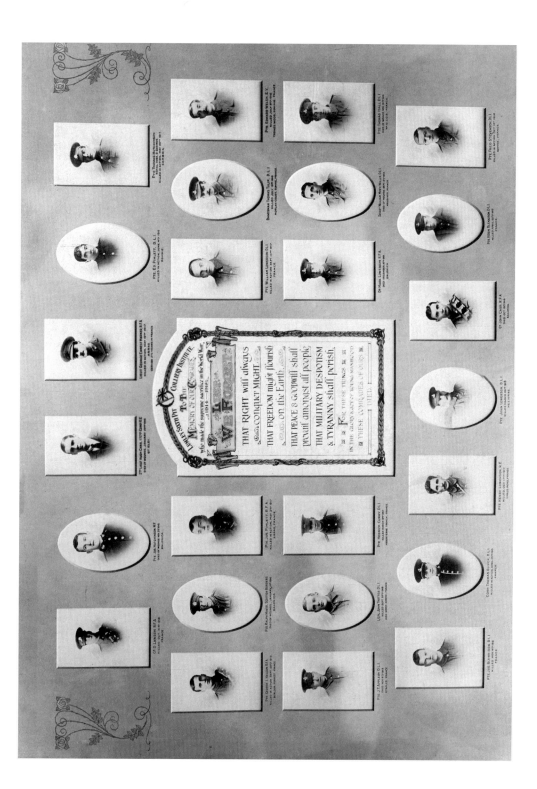

95

Miss Dorothy Coxon's Drama Group taking a break from their show 'Lilies of the Field' which they presented at the Welfare Hall, Sixth Pit in the 1950s. Dorothy Coxon is seated in the centre.

An OAP Yuletide Party, 18th December 1958.

Fence Houses people show their gratitude to their regular postman, Mr Gray, at a presentation on his retirement in May 1950.

A 'Gypsy' scene involving Lumley WI Concert Party in the 1960s. Front row: Betty Mason, Nan Willis, Jenny Lowery, Phil Willis, Brenda Garner, Jenny Macbrayne, Lena Oliver and Florrie Fenwick. Back row: Maggie Haigh, Maisie Tones, Jenny Pimlett, Linda Dunn, Peggy Howe, Mary Clark, Bessie Henderson, Bet Bainbridge, Florrie Welsh, Sadie Passmore, Lily Watkins and Elsie Fenn.

The formal opening of Lumley Community Centre in 1971. From left to right: Richard Pimlett, George Peart, Harry Suggett and Betty Temple.

Enjoying the sunshine outside the Community Centre in the 1970s. Left to right: Henderson Lowerson, John Cairns, Mr Combie, Mr Robson, Mr Herdman and Joe Cornell.

Men of the community in the Lumley Room in 1971. Back row: Eric Thompson, Thomas Agnew, Charles Lamb, John Kearney, Keith Garner, Henderson Lowerson and Stuart Wilkie. Front row: George Peart, Harry Suggett and Richard Pimlett.

Lady members of the Community Centre, 1971. Back row: Dorothy Mather, unknown, Dorothy Lamb, Dorothy Birleson, Maureen Hopkins, Tess Scullion, Alwin Gleghorn, Hannah McBride, Mrs Jones, Betty Temple, Ann Jefferson, Mary Suggett, Mrs Watson and Mrs Avery. Front row: unknown, Pat Garrity, unknown, Wendy Garrard, unknown and Edith Barker.

Lumley pensioners in tea-party mood, *circa* 1970s. Included are: Bella Hann, Mrs Preston, Mrs Wardhaugh, Mrs Watson, Mr Watson, Mrs Preece, Eva Brown, John Hunter, Edith Ingram, Nancy Craggs, Mrs Cummings, Mrs Patterson, Mr Pescod, Mrs Avery, Tommy Romaine, Betty Mason, Joe Howes and Margaret Jones.

New Year's Eve party held in the Scout's Hall (Robert Foster House) Fence Houses in the late 1970s. It was dressing up time and then guessing who?

It sure is thirsty work celebrating the arrival of a brand New Year. Once again the Scout's Hall is the venue.

Like I said – it sure is thirsty work!

A Lumley bride Margaret (Peg) Brice (née Bell) with her husband Charles (Charlie) Brice after their wedding at Christ Church, Great Lumley on 1st August 1931.

The wedding group of Stephanie (née Wilson) and Philip Lewins taken in front of Finchale Terrace, Woodstone Village, Fence Houses in the early 1940s.

The wedding group of Rona Cowan (née Curry) and Gordon Cowan outside of Christ Church, Great Lumley after their wedding in 1950.

The wedding of Eddie Horsley (Lumley footballer) and Miss Elliott in March 1950, surrounded by footballing friends. Four generations are shown in this group.

The first double wedding at Christ Church, Lumley. Mr Ernest Sweeting and Mrs Nancy Sweeting (née Brice) and Mr J. McKitten and Mrs Iris McKitten (née Brice) were married on 31st March 1951.

Wedding group of Sandra (née Nelson) and George Smith taken outside of Christ Church, Great Lumley in 1969.

A photo of the bride, Sandra Smith (née Nelson) taken outside of Christ Church, Great Lumley in 1969. In the background to the right is the old Lumley school.

Looking back into the church after their wedding in October, 1972 are: Helen Wilson (née Curry) and Stuart Wilson at Christ Church, Great Lumley.

Sheila Ellison (née Sweeting) and Fred Ellison after their wedding at Christ Church, Great Lumley on 18th June 1977.

John and Louise Taylor cutting their Golden Wedding cake at home in Fence Houses after partying with their family and friends in 1985.

PEOPLE

Mr Bob Fisher, a well-known local resident of Lumley relaxing with his dog outside the Warriors Arms, 2001.

Four generations of a Fence Houses family: Great Grandfather Curry, Grandfather Thomas Curry, Father William Curry and Baby Thomas Curry, *circa* 1916.

Herbert Fenny with his dog outside his back door in Lumley in the early 1900s.

A group of menfolk of Great Lumley, *circa* 1930s. John Hope, Adam Elliott, John Calvert, George Allan, Tom Robson, Tom Farnsworth and Kenneth Melvin.

Most of the passengers on this charabanc trip from Fence Houses in the 1920s were related to or employed by the Fence Houses branch of the Chester-le-Street Co-operative and Industrial Society Limited.

Lumley Special Constables. Included are: Jack Tindale, Mr Hutchinson, Mr Stevens and Billy Hope.

A group of members of Lumley Christ Church, *circa* 1925. Included are: Maggie Turnbull, Hannah Driver, Mary Ellen Gardiner, Mr Purvis, Reverend Ellison, Jane Powney, Bob Miller, Mrs Tindale, Harry Graham, Mrs Dodds, Mr Cowan, Miss Turnbull, Miss Fry, Miss Macdonald, Miss Shields, Mima Miller, Ethel Stevenson, Mary Ann Wilson, Mrs Cowan, Mrs Layburn, Ella Conn and Mrs Moore.

Fence Houses girl, Hilda Yellowley in 1942.

Seen in his Royal Air Force uniform, Fence Houses lad, Edward Charlton, 1942.

Two Fence Houses friends stand shoulder to shoulder in the 1940s. On the right, Mary Armstrong (in uniform) and Greta Moody.

Fence Houses family, Emma and Edward Charlton with their children and grandchildren on a Seaside trip in 1949.

Bradley Metcalf and Roy Curry of Fence Houses start motoring early in June 1950.

Young Enid Curry explores the vehicle while proud dad, Tom Curry, looks on in Fence Houses in 1953.

'Anything you can do I can do better.' William Yellowley from Fence Houses with his grand-daughter Denise Wilson, 1955.

Members of Lumley Womens'
Institute. Included are: Mrs
Celia Patterson, Mrs Lena
Oliver, Mrs Nora Ramshaw,
Mrs Skelton, Mrs Francis
Ramshaw, Miss Sally Craggs,
Mrs Agnes Swinney, Mrs
Nellie Battey, Mrs Doris
Fenny, Mrs Jenny Pimlett, Mrs
Roughley, Mrs G. Brown, Mrs
Welsh, Mrs Lee, Mrs Tait, Mrs
Jenny Lowery, Mrs Maggie
Haigh, Mrs Glendenning, Mrs
Haigh, Mrs Gladys Swinney,
Mrs Polly Lewis and Mrs
Florence Pimlett.

Mr D. Potts, Mr T. Hayley, Mr
J. Melvin and Mr L. Maddison
enjoy a break at Lumley
Terrace in the early 1950s.

Bob Johnson of Pinewood Street, Fence Houses, holding the banjo and Jimmy Smith of Sydney Street, Fence Houses, with his drum kit in the 1950s.

A group of members of Lumley Thicks chapel with their Minister. Included are: Ernie Gardiner, Jimmy Richardson Jnr, Eddie Turnbull, Ann Richardson, Mrs Noreen Forth, Mrs Richardson, Mrs Forster, Mrs Robson, Mrs Moore, Miss Dawson, Mr Johnson, Mr Davison, Mr W. Forth, Jimmy Richardson, George Carr, the Reverend Minister, Nancy Grant, Mr Long and Matty Holland.

Ladies of Lumley British Legion, *circa* 1956. Back row: Peggy Agnew, Effie Ward, Gwen Mills and Mary Peart. Middle row: Amy Brown, Margaret Anderson, Annie Huntley, Maud Johnson, Enid Wilson, Mrs McClenning and Mrs Calvert. Front row: Hannah Hoarse, Nelly Avery, Hannah Johnson and Mrs Fergerson. Possibly a Choral group?

A group of overmen, deputies and shotfirers from Lumley Sixth Pit Colliery having a get together at the Scotch Corner Hotel. Standing: Andrew Leadbitter, J. Ivison, W. Pattinson, G. Lowerson, Cyril Atkinson and J. Lowerson. Seated: W. Carr, Jack Bowes, Norman Pimlett, Jack Barnes, Fred Combey and unknown.

Bill Tindale on the left and Basil Elliott on right with their dogs at Middle Farm, Lumley. Houses now occupy this site.

Opening of the Aged People's Shelter at Fence Houses by Councillor N. Yarrow, Chairman of Chester-le-Street Rural Council (front row on the right) in September 1959.

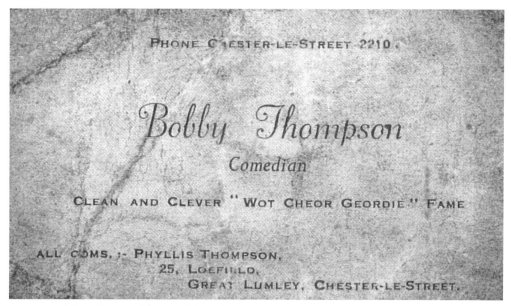

PHONE CHESTER-LE-STREET 2210.

Bobby Thompson

Comedian

CLEAN AND CLEVER " WOT CHEOR GEORDIE " FAME

ALL COMS. :- PHYLLIS THOMPSON,
25, LOEFIELD,
GREAT LUMLEY, CHESTER-LE-STREET.

A copy of local comedian Bobby Thompson's visiting card.

A group of Lumley British Legion Ladies outside of the Blacksmith's Shop at Gretna Green in the mid 1950s. They are: Nellie Baker, Florrie Kendal, Maureen Cole, Jenny Hutchinson, Nellie Ross, Mrs Hoarse, Mrs Bewley, Mrs Kendal, Mary Wells and Iris McKitten.

Mr Ernie Sweeting of Woodstone Terrace, Fence Houses proudly shows the trout he caught while fishing in 1980.

A group of Lumley residents enjoying a trip to Torquay in May 1981.

'Breathalyser test Sir?' Louise
Taylor giving Ernie Sweeting the
'test' in party mood in the late
1980s.

Before we leave the villages of Great Lumley and Fence Houses, let us have a few final glimpses of the area's most famous landmark – Lumley Castle.

A view of Lumley Castle, *circa* 1905.

A general view of Lumley Castle, *circa* 1910.

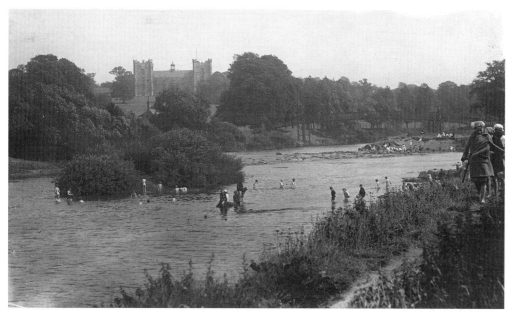

Lumley Castle overlooking the River Wear.

Print of Lumley Castle, *circa* 1831.

Footbridge and walled gardens, Lumley Castle.

Gateway to Lumley Castle.

Gates at the main entrance to Lumley Castle.

The well courtyard, Lumley Castle.

THE PEOPLE'S HISTORY

THE PEOPLE'S HISTORY
FENCE HOUSES, LAMBTON, BURNMOOR & CHILTON MOOR
BY LENA COOPER & GEOFFREY BERRIMAN

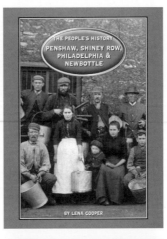

THE PEOPLE'S HISTORY
PENSHAW, SHINEY ROW, PHILADELPHIA & NEWBOTTLE
BY LENA COOPER

THE PEOPLE'S HISTORY
HOUGHTON-LE-SPRING
BY GEOFFREY BERRIMAN

THE PEOPLE'S HISTORY
CHESTER-LE-STREET
THE TWENTIETH CENTURY
BY DOROTHY A. HALL & GEORGE NAIRN

THE PEOPLE'S HISTORY
AROUND WASHINGTON
BY STUART MILLER & GEORGE NAIRN

THE PEOPLE'S HISTORY
IMAGES OF SEAHAM
BY TREVOR WILLIAMSON

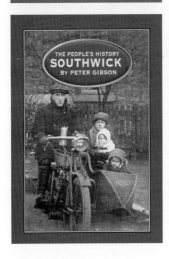

THE PEOPLE'S HISTORY
SOUTHWICK
BY PETER GIBSON

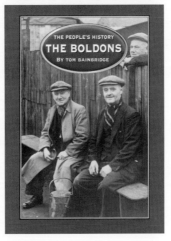

THE PEOPLE'S HISTORY
THE BOLDONS
BY TOM BAINBRIDGE

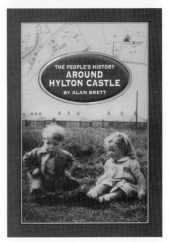

THE PEOPLE'S HISTORY
AROUND HYLTON CASTLE
BY ALAN BRETT

THE PEOPLE'S HISTORY
SOUTH SHIELDS SCRAPBOOK
BY JOHN CARLSON & JOYCE CARLSON

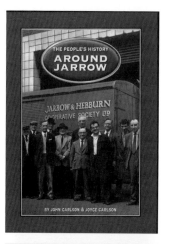

THE PEOPLE'S HISTORY
AROUND JARROW
BY JOHN CARLSON & JOYCE CARLSON

THE PEOPLE'S HISTORY
IMAGES OF SOUTH SHIELDS
BY JOHN CARLSON & JOYCE CARLSON

THE PEOPLE'S HISTORY
SUNDERLAND 'TIL I DIE
BY ALAN BRETT & ANDREW CLARK

THE PEOPLE'S HISTORY
THE TURNPIKE ROAD
SUNNISIDE MARLEY HILL BYERMOOR
BY F.G. NEWMAN WITH SUNNISIDE HISTORY SOCIETY

THE PEOPLE'S HISTORY
STANLEY REMEMBERED
BY ALAN MORRISON & JACK SLAIN

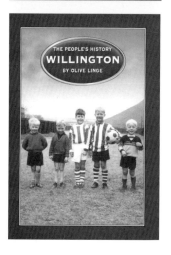

THE PEOPLE'S HISTORY
WILLINGTON
BY OLIVE LINGE

THE PEOPLE'S HISTORY
CONSETT THE PAST RELIVED
BY THE DERWENTDALE LOCAL HISTORY SOCIETY

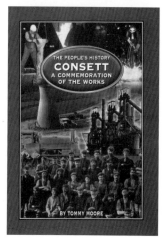

THE PEOPLE'S HISTORY
CONSETT A COMMEMORATION OF THE WORKS
BY TOMMY MOORE

The formal opening of the Great Lumley Community Centre by County
Councillor R. Pimlett on Friday, 4th June 1971.

The People's History

To order a book in The People's History series send
a cheque or postal order to:

The People's History
Suite 1
Byron House
Seaham Grange Business Park
Seaham
County Durham
SR7 0PY

All books are £9.99 and postage and packaging is free.

Cheques and postal orders made payable to The People's History Ltd.